portraits
poems by e.p.rose

Published in the United States by
Studio on 41 Press
Galisteo, New Mexico
galisteoliz.com

Poems and Artwork: Elizabeth Rose
Book Design: Donna Brownell

Printed in the U.S.A.

Copyright© 2016 by Elizabeth Rose.
All rights reserved.

No part of this publication may be reproduced, stored in a retrieval system or transmitted in any form or by any means, electronic, mechanical, photocopying, recording, or otherwise without the prior written permission of the copyright holder, except brief quotations used in a review.

ISBN 978-0-9861188-5-2

for
David

David

when
I read the poem
of your face
beside me on the pillow
the world spins beautiful

birth

attracted by first cries of worldly breath
black panther came to guide my path
blinked yellow lantern-eyes
witnessed my arrival
lamplight's shadow dance
the snow-pillowed Himalayan jungle

spat from her womb
my mother birthed me
one brief moment we connected
I struggled to fix her face within my focus

after she no longer had milk to give
I thanked her for my life
separated   strangers

discovery

my fingers gently part the green   expose wild
strawberries clustered above a Kashmiri snow-fed
brook   surprise my tongue with their sweetness

in those woods of rhododendron and pine poke
tiny trefoils wood sorrel nestled at their mossy
feet   I nibble one tasting lemon

deeper between closed forest firs   lurid red and
white spotted toadstools promise eternal rest
lure me to take a bite   but I am not tempted

above the tree-line below the snow stands a
solitary birch   pale parchment shredding from
its trunk   for raven to scribe his story

I step into a knee-high carpet of gentians beside
a snowdrift pitted with imprints where a yeti
passed last winter on his quest towards the sun

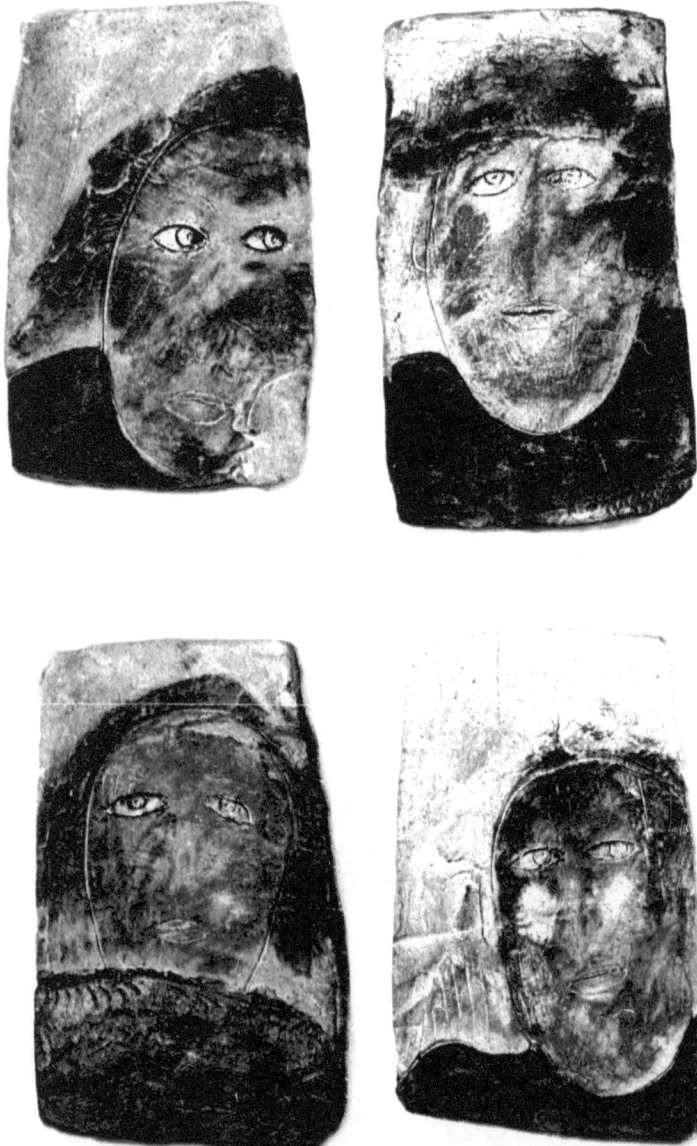

and I saw Everest

get out of the car

> shaken from sleep
> I shiver on a hairpin's bend
> thin cotton dress flapping
> shielded in my father's grip
> he points skyward

fix this in your mind   always

> however hard I looked
> not comprehending
> it's land mass rooted in the plain
> child eyes saw only a sail shaped cloud
> above the tulle
> skirting the Himalayan range

look   the highest mountain in the world

> I rubbed my eyes
> and in the blue
> I saw the floating ship
> Everest

a wake up call

a traveling circus dragged into Sorga's dust bowl
one Indian afternoon when I was six
spilled elephant dung   tiger smell
a Himalayan bear straining on his chain

in a front seat   a pukkha missy-sahiba
in a smocked lawn-cotton frock
I fidgeted waiting for drums to roll
for tumblers to fill the sawdust
the crack of the ringmaster's whip

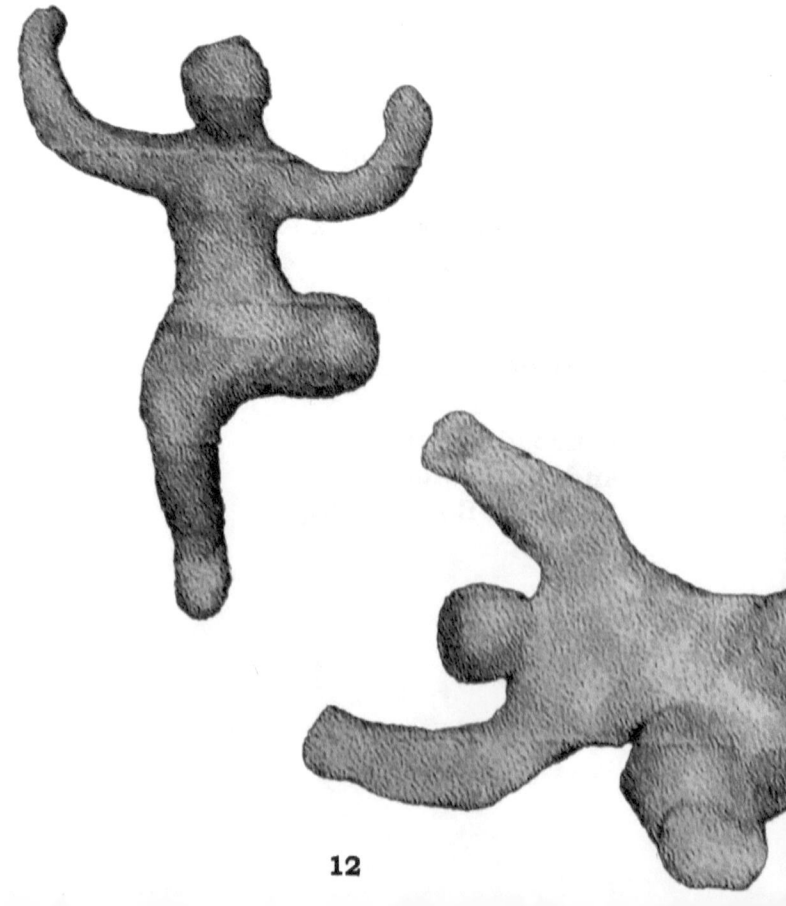

a trumpet blares
a girl my age in tinsel leotards   lips gaudy red
bends backwards   head between her legs
lopes crab-like towards my ringside seat
chin cupped in her hands

she shakes herself undone
springs cartwheels onto her father's shoulders
eyes fixed on pink candy-floss sticky in my hand
I saw then she was working   not having fun

swinging high on a trapeze she vanished
left tent ropes dangling

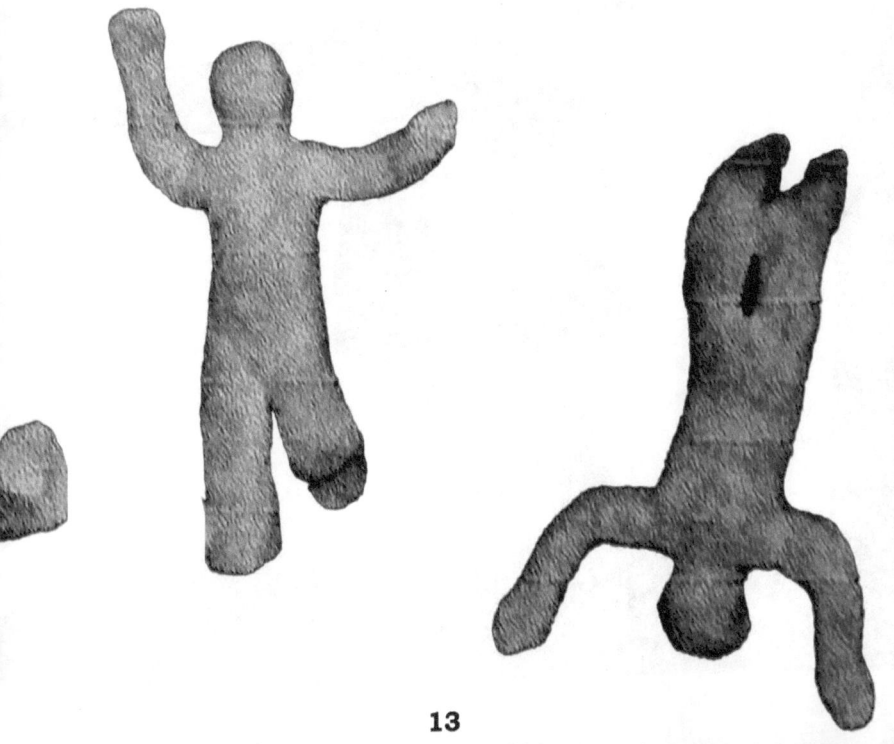

my childhood pet

Bertha died of twisted puppies
she's buried in the garden my mother said

Max   Bertha's doggy husband and I
held vigil over her hiding place underground
hoping for her muddy nose to reappear
nudge wetly on my bare leg
her playful woof

Bertha my shadow   my best friend

she pleaded her dachshund best
to climb the apricot tree
her paw scratching on the bark
below where I lay draped
along an upper branch
sucking furry skinned orange fruit
and spitting stones for her to chase
teasing *Bertha Bertha come*

all day
Max sleeps
I play alone

flying dream

all childhood long
I believed
if you thought you could
you could
fly that is
not flapping
not with wings
undulate behind the clouds

each eyelid-shuttered night
I hovered mid-air above a treetop rookery
battled headwinds to reach I don't know where
knowing only I must arrive
before daylight grounded me

by day
confident
I practiced
launched from the bed rail
belly flopped onto the mattress ticking

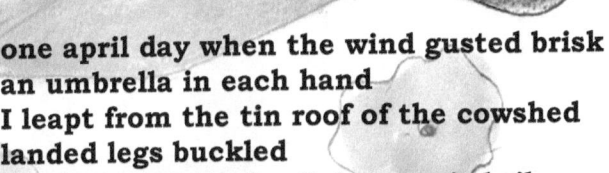

the barest second
I really did
I swear
I flew

one april day when the wind gusted brisk
an umbrella in each hand
I leapt from the tin roof of the cowshed
landed legs buckled
tangled with the brolly's mangled ribs

but... if I tried hard enough to hold myself aloft...
I could... I know I could... fly

a look back

I remember her   the child
index finger horns pointy on her head a billy-goat
unafraid inside a druid's stone circle
she bounds the moor crushing purple heather
feels the wind's wild comb un-tangle her hair

balanced on one leg atop Kestor's granite outcrop
I'm the King of the Castle she sings
to no one for no reason   to feel song's quiver
strike   not a bull's eye but a raven's

a snapshot in a shoe box
a faded lifetime stares back
the girl who once was me   is me   shameless
her skirt   was it orange?   hitched
into her knicker-elastic
grazed kneecap from her clamber up an oak tree
her oak tree home in Half-Acre field   where
one summer lifetime   she watched four sky blue
speckled eggs unaware her touch had addled
them   no robin chicks would ever pierce the
fragile shells

I close the lid   I am no longer her   but a memory

Emma my Granny Rose

tell me granny
I want to hear

ten childish fingers
rest lightly on your knees
read unspoken pages from your face
penned across eighty years and four
wait   silent to be told

    ramrod-straight tucked tight in your wheelchair
    the tartan rug that binds your lap cannot stem
    the spools
    of remembered Himalayan summers un-laced
    your bareback ride to the spice-scented Champa

    viper hiss
    a baby swelled your belly
    banished   torn from your lover
    shipped to Liverpool's weeping skies
    alone never again to see your homeland

I am not fooled
by your whale-boned face
ploughed by age
prayer book sallow in your hand

I see the secrets braided in your hair
the waltz your feet spin
the lock of his illicit gaze

before death claims you granny
tell me

tell me your tale
the story that begins
once upon a time...a long long time ago
I was born in the jungle on the floor in the ruins
of a Hindu temple...

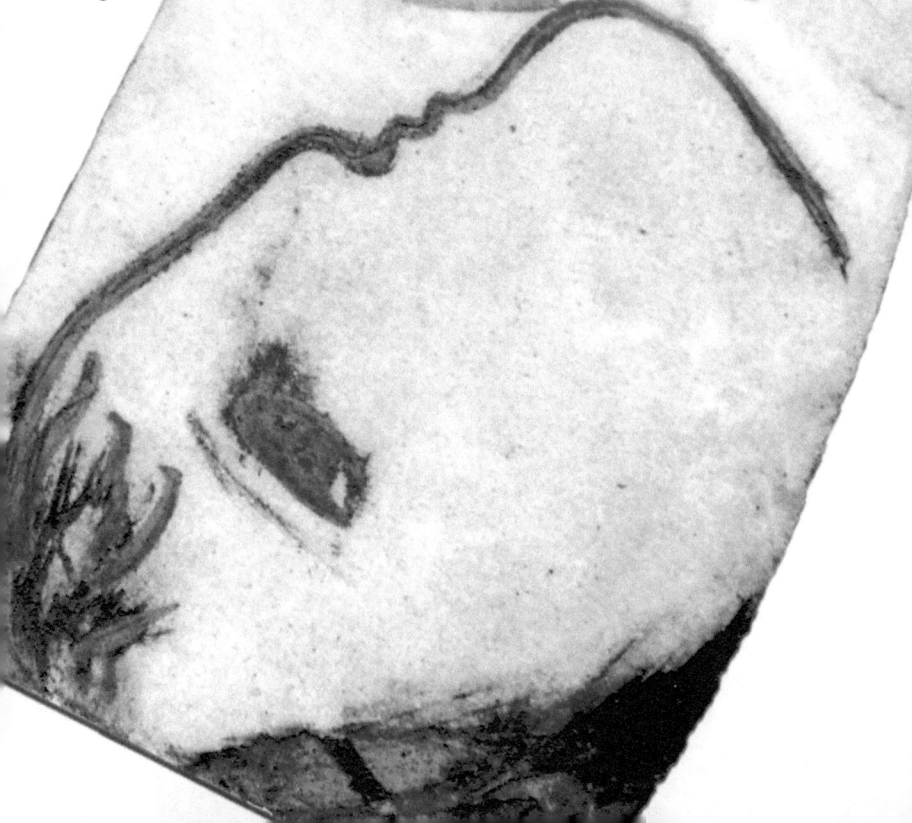

digging

what are you doing? I asked
I am digging for my roots she answered
puzzled *will you find them buried?* I persisted
of course she nodded *they're holding up this tree*
and pointed where the Beech tree's silver trunk
exploded green into blue

that's my home
that's me
I am the tree

she put down her spade
sat beside me
pressed my hand against the bark
feel she insisted *I am alive*

and handed me her spade
now you dig she encouraged
turning I found myself alone

skylight bird

what did she want to say
peering through our skylight
her raven's belly feathers
pressed to its unyielding dome
she spread her wings
fussed her twigless nest
to lay her prophecies

if she laid them
I never saw the yoke trail
heard the message
before she cawed
flew away
left us gazing
skyward

small print

something was awry that morning

half-eaten tins and dirty pans spilled tomato paste on every surface littered evidence of my husband's unremembered midnight feasting

catch him before he slips away

sticky-wet where he peed yellow rivers against the wall outside my bedroom   woke me with its streaming

deep down he must hate me

it's the new way to take blood pressure   he stood rocking   a wire coat hanger swinging from one arm   fingers pressed lightly on his pulse

our dam of twenty years was crumbling stone by stone

on holiday in Sri Lanka he urged   look behind you at those people in dinner jackets with ice skates on their heads

they've gone now I comforted staring at the grove of shimmering palms

cross-legged quietly on my bed I shut my eyes prayed *help me my sweet lover is drowning in his Parkinsonian sea*

an unseen angel whispered *check his medication*

I bowed my head   waited for a lucid moment to
tell my madman he was mad   I took his hands
pretend I told my doctor husband   *your patient
is behaving oddly*

he fell silent   checked the phial's smallest print
….in some cases …..hallucinations may occur
one pill less   day by day   he cut his medication
'til coconuts grew again on trees and ice skates
melted

let's dance   he offered me a sprig of jasmine
cheated death

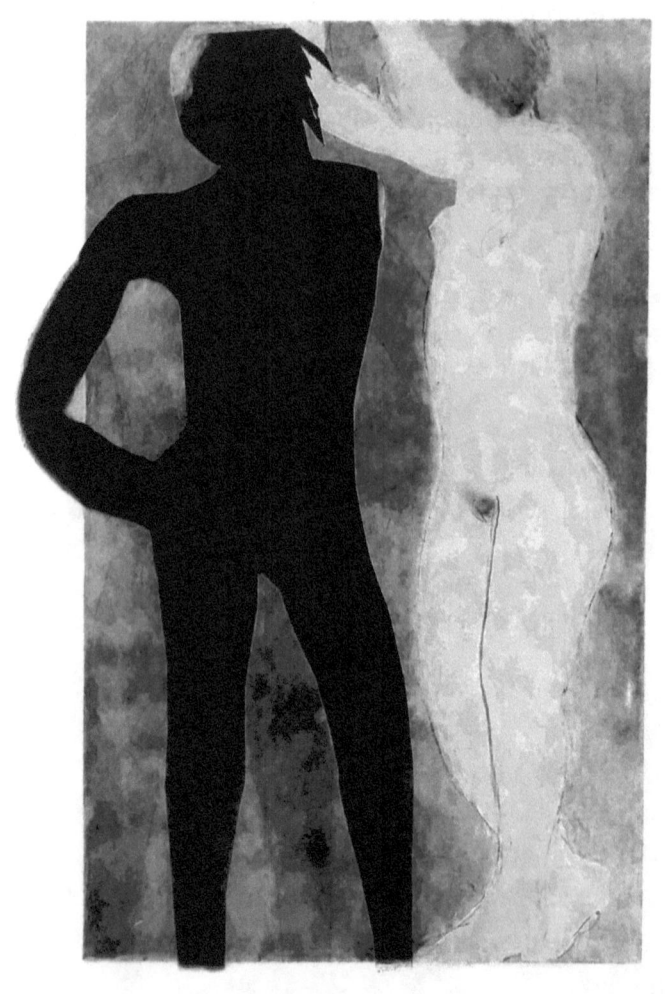

tomorrow

tomorrow when I lie alone
when no shirts of his lie crumpled on the floor
when one plate stares empty on the table
and the porch hammock swings empty

I will wish...
I will weep
I will pine for him

stare into the laundry basket
seek his grubby shorts to add to my wash
search vainly for his missing sock

today
he snores beside me
snuffling in his sleep
I smile   thankful he is with me still

listening for your return

seeking you each morning
my ear pressed against your door
I strain for the slow shuffle-scrape
your slippers etch across the flagstone floor

cobwebs bind shut the windows
shield the yellowed tablecloth's
two places expectant on the kitchen table

no aromatic vapor escapes the iron casserole
its half-moon handle
worn smooth by so much lifting
hangs cold   lifeless on the hob

each visit the cottage sinks
and I must bend lower...
part ivy tendrils

fearing a hollow echo
I hesitate before I let drop
the brass knocker we chose together
before   without a word
you vanished that Thursday evening
two long months ago

did a blackberry vine
tumble you into the river
sweep you downstream
face turned hawk-ward to the gold hidden in the
sinking sun

come my love

I obey your whisper
rest my ax against the wall
stack *piñon* newly cut in the willow
basket I wove for you last winter

white tail

did you visit me last night
gaze through the window
while I was sleeping
your hoof prints tell me you were here

I tracked your two-toed path across the garden
to the fence where you jumped higher than the moon
gouging holes in the dust where you landed

I saw tiny indentations beside yours
did you bring your newborn fawn to show him
a two legged human   caged inside four walls
slumbering beneath my cloud

September's full moon harvest

beneath night's coverlet she
skipped the garden path
twirled apples on a string
offered me a bite

your prize she crooned
her smile spilled seeds
discarded cores

        she loved me once
        why else knit one plain one pearl
        sew six red buttons down the front
        match hers to mine

September's full moon bled the sun
my mother's disappearing tracks
dangled half-chewed apples

a hanky fluttered
I was four
unable to sing

house mouse—t'was but a dream

kleenex-wrapped
dead   a mouse lies in my jacket pocket
hidden   to save my phobic friend hysterics

proud   she showed me round her newly
purchased home
I spotted the creature feet up
immobile on her pin-clean kitchen floor
quickly scooped it out of sight

forgetting
at the front door of my home
my fingers curled about something not a key
I flung the tissue-shrouded corpse heavenward
watched it plummet into a scream filled puddle

Makima's mountain

each time I drive Tijeras Canyon to Albuquerque
I slow to sixty miles an hour
scan Sandia's recumbent outline
search for her grass bed ruffled by dew
—Makima's last resting place

she lay down   a fresh daisy chain coiled about
her wrist
a photo of her teacher clamped to her heart
a note pinned to her chest read *my name is
Makima do not grieve*

Baba's called me home Makima informed her
Catholic sons the week before
oh mother   I beg you   p-lease they groaned

*thursday   Guru's day   that's when I leave   I
bought myself a white silk blouse*
she chimed   deaf to their distress

Sandia's peak was dark when Makima chanted
her last prayer
as dawn tip-toed the horizon   she caught her
breath
sad to be leaving Earth   her home for seventy-
six years

Makima tightened her Indian cashmere shawl
cast its embroidered flowers the length of
Sandia's crest
chose a nest bathed in watermelon red

ten days the search party combed the mountain
prodded every clump   each chamisa bush

they found her lying on her back   the sky
reflected in her eyes
flesh firm   pink   beatified
scent of roses clung to her

now   approaching Sandia Mountain from the East
I picture you sleeping   Makima
think how God called you home

her autopsy reads *death from natural causes*

flash in the pan

I bought a goldfish a week ago
in exchange for my eleven dollars sixty cents
received   one glass bowl   a shaker of fish food
a green plastic weed sealed in cellophane

as a change from TV   first thing home
for five whole evenings I sat watching
bonding with my new pet   chimed *kutchi-koo*
in a high-pitched fish-friendly tone

mummsie's home

round it sped snapping up the crumbs I sprinkled
one more chance I growled   tapped its glass
not once did my pet pause   make eye contact
I flushed the damn thing down the toilet

brush scarlet

brush scarlet poppies on my forehead
paint a bluebell wood inside my head
drown images I wish I'd never seen

a stepped pyramid of stone
where Apollo's Temple
dominates ancient Nimes
proclaims the tourist crown

I emerge from Cesar's inner sanctum
adjust to the glare   wonder
at the Roman city mapped below
a flight of steps unprotected by rail

I draw back my foot
from the stairway that isn't there
inch down the way I came tread by narrow tread

a silent crowd gathered

below the trompe l'oeil staircase
a jumble of odd angled arms and legs
a woman's shoe
pocket purse
a young life
splash the pavement
bleed the agony of her friends

brush scarlet poppies on my forehead
paint a bluebell wood
drown me dreamless in sleep

better red than blue?

stripped   their skin walnut brown no longer
feared wind's fiery breath   the youth and fair-
haired girl trod deep into White Sands Monument
their quest—survive one full night and day

before they left   between fronds of tamarisk in
the creek bed below their yurt   each picked a
pebble that sang their song   saliva-inducing to
moisten swollen tongues
sweat saltlick

dawn   silk dunes   yucca   goose-bump shadows
he became invisible to her   she to him
she drew a sundial with her heel   marked the
sun   to see nothing—her goal

eyes closed   veined red velvet encased her
owl-eyed   unblinking   her world swam
transparent   spiraled cerulean light beads

whorls Hokusai depicted in his etchings   that
each saw what the other was seeing she knew
then space and sky held no emptiness

her own footprints led back to where she'd left
the youth   standing   arms spread scarecrow
wide   she touched his chest   her finger
testing he was real

stumbling upon the feathered remnants of a kill
gutted   leather-dry
he plucked and placed three wing-plumes in her
hair   fringed her eyes
she poked three into his curls

hunkered in the shade pool scooped earlier from
a purple slope below the surface of the dune
they wove two feather caps   padded them with
speckled buzzard-down
insulated their brains against the arcing sun

fixated on imagined desert pools   hearing
water splash   they turned their faces to drink
delirious   slug-fatted tongues   sometimes
panting   wild for death   they struggled to keep
from running   screaming

breath in   breath out   eyes shut—see red   eyes
open—blue   day blinded silver-white

I am a stupid fool   I am a stupid fool   three
thousand lines the youth mouthed
is red better than blue?   blue better than red?
her question   with the pebble in her mouth
tumbled round her head

Las Vegas paradise

where trees cast no shadows
and machines cascade money
I follow three Nepalese nuns
to Rome's Tivoli fountain
grey robed   cloven-sandaled feet
arm in arm they smile into a digital lens
the glory of the Himalayas back home forgotten

I saw no one stop
to point out coyote
emerging from an air vent in the marble floor
to pounce on a plaster rabbit nibbling plastic grass

a couple wanders hand in hand
beneath the sunset projected on a painted sky
breathing temperature controlled air
while coyote drags his trophy
behind a lime green tortoise
heads for Hell's exit

premonition

I have seen fish with human heads
the woman from Bolivia screamed
the world will end if we don't change

www.galisteoliz.com

www.elizabethrosesculpture.net

**also
available from
e.p.rose**

and

100 years of Colonial Rule in British India 1850-1947 through the personal stories of one family. Caught in two World Wars, pre Mutiny skirmishes, and the Great Sepoy Rebellion the true saga of lives not so "pukkha" as might be supposed. Hugh Rose's back-story exposes child marriage, social taboos, adulterous affairs over many summers in a Himalayan Hill Station, illegitimate pregnancies and banishment to England. More a poet than a soldier, Hugh, a British Officer of the Raj, serves with the 3rd Queen Alexandra's Own Gurkha Rifles in the Kyber Pass bordering the Northwest Frontier Afghanistan. Gentlemen's sports, bandits, tribal warlords, missionaries, ordinary men and ghosts are not enough. Bored, Hugh seconds to the Political and Foreign Service in Arabia, Persia, and Waziristan, until disgraced, he is "invited" to return to his regiment after five years. A naked Colonel's dictum "conformity kills" guides Hugh's adventurous life. Partition frees both India and Hugh.

ISBN 978-0-9861188-0-7

CANCIONES CHIFLADAS

Penned daily at dawn on a Mexican beach, Elizabeth's collection of verse opens up a world of language delightful to children of all ages and those who read to them

ISBN 978-0-9863386-3-8

ISBN 978-0-9861188-4-5

www.ingramcontent.com/pod-product-compliance
Lightning Source LLC
Chambersburg PA
CBHW020628300426
44112CB00010B/1240